Between Worlds

GW00385089

Rosabelle Boswell

Langaa Research & Publishing CIG
Mankon, Bamenda

Publisher
Langaa RPCIG
Langaa Research & Publishing Common Initiative Group
P.O. Box 902 Mankon
Bamenda
North West Region
Cameroon
Langaagrp@gmail.com
www.langaa-rpcig.net

Distributed in and outside N. America by African Books Collective
orders@africanbookscollective.com
www.africanbookscollective.com

ISBN-10: 9956-552-06-2

ISBN-13: 978-9956-552-06-1

© Rosabelle Boswell 2022

All rights reserved.
No part of this book may be reproduced or transmitted in any form or by
any means, mechanical or electronic, including photocopying and
recording, or be stored in any information storage or retrieval system,
without written permission from the publisher

Photograph by Polina Tankilevitch, Moscow
Instagram: ptankilevitch

Table of Contents

Introduction

Earth is transitioning to a more volatile future, where rising sea levels, the loss of marine biodiversity and increasing ocean pollution present challenges to the survival of humans and a diversity of species. Human action in the form of overpopulation, overexploitation of natural resources, rising inequality and violence is deepening the environmental crisis. The Intergovernmental Panel on Climate Change (IPCC), founded in 1988 by the United Nations Environment Programme (UNEP) and approved by 195 countries worldwide produced a report to the UN (August 2021), which indicates many environmental changes taking place across the globe. These include increased rainfall and flooding, soaring temperatures and drought, the loss of sea-based livelihoods and dwindling fish stocks. These effects are leading to starvation, increased poverty, and ecological degradation. Unless governments make the effort to reduce 'growth' and 'development', specifically the unchecked exploitation of marine (and other natural) resources, the environmental situation will not improve, and neither will the human crises of climate change. Moderate use of Earth's resources is key to achieving a more balanced global ecosystem for the benefit of all. Behavioural change forms a critical part of the environmental conservation journey. The latter requires thought and effort from all and across all cultures and social worlds.

In recent years, countries party to the UN Framework Convention on Climate Change (UNFCCC) met to discuss the immediate and long-term implications of climate change for Earth. The Community of Parties convened COP26 to discuss the current and impending climate crisis. While the COP reports and meetings clearly depict the impacts of environmental change, the long-term effects on coastal communities are yet to emerge. The impact will be widespread because nearly 60 percent of the world's population live at the coast or within 100km of the high-water mark.

This anthology forms part of a series of thoughts regarding the form, substance, place and meaning of the ocean to humans, and of the place of marine species in human life. The aim of the anthology is to address the issue of climate change by raising public awareness of the centrality, beauty and significance of the ocean, and of marine life to humanity. The goal is to induce positive behavioural change vis-à-vis the ocean by representing its undeniable value to all. Part of the anthology focuses on African coastal experiences, shedding light on ocean development plans that are negatively impacting ocean health and the integrity of small island developing states. The poems also touch on African spirituality, and Africans' connection with the oceans. Some of the thoughts expressed in the poetry are rearticulated in academic journal articles published while this anthology was in progress. Specifically, discussion on the extent to which an environmental/marine holism exists in Africa, and its potential to advance sustainable ocean management. The poems also reach beyond Africa, to consider diaspora experiences of the ocean and issues pertaining to diasporic connection across the oceans. These poems indicate the role of diaspora and global, indigenous philosophies of ocean conservation to the climate management process. Beyond the positive reflections on Africa and global, indigenous philosophies of ocean and sea, I also highlight anxieties percolating due to the continued neglect of ocean conservation and protection. Africa's participation in and contribution to the global issue of ocean health remains barely audible. Only five African heads of state attended the Climate Summit hosted by US President Joe Biden in April 2021 and in one of the most developed countries of the continent, South Africa, the youth has judged the country's Nationally Determined Contributions (NDCs) for climate change, not ambitious enough. The situation is dire and made even more so by the fact that developed states still have to action the 100 billon US Dollar climate finance pledged to developing (including African) countries in 2009.

As a creative endeavour, the poems presented here also form part of sedimented thoughts I've had about the more formal analyses of coastal identity and cultural heritages. While research sponsors like neat lines and compartmentalised projects or ideas, for 'creatives', ideas collide, combine, and produce fractalized outputs, offering glimpses of, and forms of knowledge that may not be easily 'captured' for straightforward 'accreditation'. What do we make of knowledge gathered in fields of memory, imagination, dreams, sentiment, and ritual? These are not 'fields' in the classic, anthropological sense – there are no objectively perceived realities that one can lay hold of and determine ethical conduct for. In this regard, producing this anthology has allowed parallel conversations to take place. Conversations with 'experts' in diverse fields of scientific ocean conservation and governance, as well as conversations with artists deeply embedded in aquapelagic spaces. The work as also helped me to see the possibilities of knowledge production via spaces that remain profoundly sensory but may not be perceived as 'legitimate' grounds for data collection.

The anthology is also entitled 'Between Worlds' because the collection explores the ocean as a multiply constituted world, and Earth is a place where all species live 'between worlds.' There is the aqueous, diverse enlivened substance of the ocean itself, human social and ecological relations with the oceans across different worlds, the human psychological experience of, and metaphorical expressions of ocean relations as well as post-human, cross-species relations arising from ocean 'worlds'.

The second part of the anthology is 'guided' by research in imaginary ethnography. Specifically, the imagination of worlds that do not yet exist. In a way, these poems seem to collapse space and time, offering 'case studies' of a dystopic future for Earth and humankind. Anthropologists and social geographers have long discussed the collapse of time-space on Earth, noting that industrialization and modernization have contributed to both the 'heating up' of climates and increased speed for everything else. Thus, we not only have fast food, but we are compelled into fast and immediate communication, as well as multi-situated awareness.

Drawing on the post-apocalyptic digital art of Dutch deviant artist, Arthur Haas, and imagining the worlds that he and others would likely imagine, I wrote poems to depict life on both a disastrous Earth, and on imaginary worlds to come. In this way, the anthology speaks to two projects that I am working on. One more audibly so than the other. The first is the ethnographic project on ocean cultures, heritage and conservation in Africa, and the second is a project that investigates past and future cultural heritages. The latter seeks to understand heritages in their 'traditional', currently known forms and emerging technological heritages, specifically those altering the relationship between humans and machines. Lastly, these poems are not merely for deep reflection on the sombre issue of climate change. They are meant to be savoured, to unleash the imagination, galvanise us into action for positive change and to open up new vistas, new ways of experiencing the ocean.

Escape to Pohnpei (Micronesia)

Standing on the shore
before an emerald sea
She remained quiet
breathing the soft breeze.
Below the liquid green
Mantas swam unseen
And coral gardens
blossomed, pristine.
Above, clouds hurried along
Through a blue, high sky
And the sun,
gloriously robed in light
fell upon her shoulders.
She leaned against a pandanus tree
And dreamed of another paradise
But none could compare
To Pohnpei.

Colour

Some think
The sea is blue
Turquoise Mediterranean
Arctic hue
Or a glassy Sargasso.
But the sea,
Does not agree
With you, or me.
It is golden in the sunrise,
Red, when the sun sets,
Black on moonlit nights
And silver, for sad clouds.
The sea does not care
For your colours.

The Shore

It was not pretty,
Calm, or soft
It was not even,
Not dry,
Or easy.
Tumbling with weathered stones
Covered in wet red seaweed
Washed by wavelets
Eddying through remains
Picked by greedy gulls.
I walked a barren, stony shore.
I saw it all,
Chokka boats dancing for fish
The red-aged hull of an unknown vessel
Seaweed seeds
Oystercatcher feed
Wind whipping my face and legs
Beckoning me, against all odds
To come back, again.

Sometimes

Sometimes I wonder
What it would be like
To fold myself into the ocean
Like the butter I fold into flour
Sometimes I wonder
What it would be like
To surf a wave
Like an iron surfs a shirt
Sometimes I wonder
What it would be like
To let go of expectations,
The ocean has none.

Swimming

People go to the sea
To see swimmers
Not knowing that,
Swimmers are on the shore

       ____ in their churches
       ____ in schools
       ____ and public parks
Swimmers are swimming
Against tides unknown.

Waterworld

Warm, against winter cold
Water wild, water sweet
Gather me in,
Fill me with awe,
So I no longer feel
The brittle cold,
Pull me into
Your unknown depths.

Polina Tankilevitch, *Underwater*

Sea Call

Come with me!
I yearn for you day and night.
Soon I will cease to pull you close
And no longer kiss your ankles with my cold lips.
You will dream of my kelp hair
And of my brooding dark.
In your dreams,
I will toss you in my arms,
You will remember my voice
Whispering in a conch shell
And hear me say I love you
But you will be mistaken
For,
They will take me from you.

Empty Canoes (Ghana)

Empty canoes float
In a grey lagoon
The men are gone
The dock's all forlorn
A fish-less sea
Trapped against a blue sky
No-one asked what happened
No-one remembered to ask why.

Canoe Women (Ghana)

Canoes gather for a wild festival
Of colour, joy and feasting.
Women in bright garb
Circle the canoes,
Dancing to ancient rhythms
Invoking the protection
Of spirits, swimming deep
In the Lagoon.

Lac Rose (Senegal)

Burning Sun
Salted skin
Man shining with shea butter
His torso hard from a hard life.
His young boat floats
On Lac Rose
Shoulder deep in pink water
He breaks up the salt
Dredging black diamonds.
Tonight, his family will eat well.

Oil's Well

Oil's well they say,
Limitless ocean
Fertile seas
The world's not a-stopping
Not until –
Everything's dead.
The fishermen won't cry
The fishermen won't die,
'Coz the sea is bountiful,
And oil's not a crime!
We can scour the bottom,
Muddy the top –
And when it's all dead,
When there's not a drop,
Then,
We'll stop.

After Wakashio

In the dark muddy low
Rubbery legged mangroves,
Anchor deep in the slurry.
A crab,
Two fish, and
Another creature float by,
Carried by amber water.
Days after,
After the sinking
After the hull snapped in two
After bloated dolphins washed ashore
After they sank knee deep in oil
After acrid fumes filled the air
They said the water's clean
But nothing,
Stirred beneath the surface.

The Island of Secrets

Below Diego Garcia
And far from the Mascarenes
Agalega lies forlorn,
Like the half-sister at a wedding.
But even half-sisters are appealing
In the light of a rising dawn,
A dawn of competition
In a sea awash with heavy history.
Quickly buildings rise,
As do runways longing for
B57s, Submarines and oil rigs.
It's a new dawn for Agalega
And its people wait,
Not knowing if,
Eviction is planned.

Knowing her Secrets (Mauritius)

Everyone thinks they know her
The contours of her coast
Her forests deep within
Her waterfalls, shy,
Only fall if they peep,
But her sumptuous hills
Rolling down to the beach
Do beguile…
They roll without care
In tropical air
Relinquishing all,
To white sand
Where her wiles lay bare.

The Pirate

He was not a pirate
But a farmer
Whose lands were taken
And world, shaken.
When he opened his eyes
He was at sea
Tossed about with others
On a rough deck
They told him,
"You're a pirate now"

Sakatia (Madagascar)

I crossed an unremarkable sea
To reach a sacred island
An island of impenetrable green
An island of ancient ancestors
And even older stories
There,
I met three wise women
Who told me of braided love,
Of orchids and perfumes
The sacredness of all islands
I did not understand
Until I looked into their eyes
And saw my ancestors.

Sails Right By

The curious sight
Of sails in the distance
Makes me wonder –
Who is on deck?
Are his arms holding her tight?
Does she feel safe?
Or is she at the helm,
Steering a ship
Alone,
Into a wondrous new dawn?

Sailin' Feelin'

Standing on the shore
He looked out to sea
Remembering the feelin'
Of sailin' on air.
Catamaran aloft
Tilted to the side
Waves flying to catch
His hair tipping down.
White water rising
Hull pushed up high
He held on to memories
Of the sailin' feelin.

The Catch

Early morn'
I rise to sea
To catch my tea
The sea sees me
And laughs a wave
Damn it, too late
The sea,
Caught me.

Rain on Sea

Silver sky
Leaden clouds
Dripping rain
On a slate sea.
No bird stirs
No boat breaches
Whitened waves
Frothing high.
She dives in
Surprising onlookers.

Island Girl

Cheese in her pocket
Sand in her hair
Born on a pearl
In a vast open sea
She opened her eyes
While a volcano slept
And a hurricane raged.
She did not change,
Not for you,
Or me.

The Diver

A kind sky
Stretched above him
And good soil
Held his feet.
Perfection,
He reached high
Hands pointed to
That kind sky
Body arched
Heels off the ground
He flew –
Arms wide
Sleekly knifing
Into the Zanzibari sea.

The Sculptor

He did not remember
How he first learned to carve.
His mother told him that in a dream
It had come to him.
The prophesied blessing of ancestors
So, he sat each day,
On a stone, overlooking the sea
Of Bagamoyo
Carving the inspiration of his father
And his father's father.

Harbour

An unremarkable harbour
Lay ahead –
Surrounded in morning mist
Bobbing buoys and silky seals.
A sailor looked out –
Over the bow,
Peering into the oily sea
He shed a tear,
But it floated on a slick.

Two Boats (South Africa)

In the dock –
Two boats floated
On a murky sea.
The one sighed to the other
And said,
"Sweet neighbour, when shall we sail together?
We remain in the dock
With your bow touching mine
Like sweet lips on a glass
Of irresistible wine."
His neighbour turned to him and replied,
"Dear neighbour, we are but friends,
Docked side by side
Our friendship is not made for kisses,
Or wine."

The Deep

It is dark in the deep
Where life does not sleep
Where eyes glow
And flimsy limbs float
On heated vent flows
All is light
In the heavy below,
Unimaginable span
Unfathomable form
In the dark deep
Life does not sleep
Eyes and limbs float
And stomachs secrets keep.

Deep Sea Water

Deep Below
In darkness deep
A thousand leagues beneath
The fish do not sleep.
In glorious array
They dance and play,
Far, far away
From humans who prey.
No hand shall reach
In the dark beneath.
Only eyes can stare
The eyes of those
Who dare.

Surface Lies

Dancing legs pulse
Blousy top undone
Tells a sparkling lie.
Breach the surface,
Search beneath
There, the truth lies
On its side
Releasing a thousand cries.
Jellyfish passing by are blind,
They live to sting
And love to lie.

Low Tide

Low tide
Boys' Pride
Take Sides
No Cries,
No Sighs
No lies
Just Glide
Net
The Prize

The Reef

I remember the reef
Off Ile Bernache
A cerulean sea
Cupped by powder sand
The reef so still
All the little fish danced.

The Bend

She went with it
The wave.
It lifted her up
Off the ocean floor
So fast
Her breath did not last.
He was there at the top
A tiny fish
Tossed about by the sea,
Together they gave up
And gave in,
To the bend.

Little Pool

Little pool all alone
Waiting for the tumbling surf
Gather all the pebbles lost
Along this wild shore
Tuck them in –
Sigh them to sleep
Shield them from fury
Unleashed by the tide
Until the end of time.

Beyond Our Imagination

If a thousand pebbles
Rumble along our shores
And a thousand limpets
Cling to them more,
If a thousand waves
And a thousand ripples
Make their way
Up this beach
Their reasons for doing so
Would still be,
Beyond our imagination.

Cabo Delgado

In the north of the south
Where the sun burns bright,
A green blue sea flows.
Politicians cry
That they are not to blame
They are not the ones
Who have set the coast aflame,
The guns come
Men surly in green
Masked,
Arrive,
They steal all dignity.

Plastic

Arriving below
I find you bare
Your sandy body unadorned
Of coral jewels.
I find no pearl necklaces
Or tight clam safes.
Instead,
I find
Plastic chandeliers
Unchanging
For a thousand years.

Salt

I could lick you
Or let you sting my eyes
Dissolve and drink you
Take you deep inside
But you're already there,
Dancing in my bones,
Wrapped around my heart,
Don't ever leave me,
Salt.

The Ngalawa (Zanzibar)

Sleek in cool waters
Unknown in the west
the ngalawa cuts into the wind
the breath of generations
Hold it afloat.
Beneath, ropes that bound,
unwind.
Ancestors rise
crying, rasping
they tell it where to sail.
The ngalawa listens
And glides through dark waters
to a rising sun.

Fetch

Go to the shore
Where the waters churn
And the sand boils
With the tide.
The sea has a gift
It cannot hide.
Fetch it for me
That sparkling slippery trophy
After, we shall make our way home
Through dark days
Side by side

Island

She was an island
In her mind
Separated from other atolls
floating about the sea.
She had no-one to talk to
No-one to understand
the flotsam and jetsam
surfing waves
or pulled by the moon.
Off her shores
Fish danced in wild abandon
chattering to each other
in bubbles that bloomed
under the surface
But she,
alone,
hemmed in by the tides
was alone.
In her mind,
with no-one to speak back
to the tsunami
rising off,
the island.

Ama

(Sea Woman, Japan)
I am Ama
Whose prize is not the sea
But the pearl in her bosom
Cold though she be
I seek her dark comfort
Her jewel shining in the midnight ocean
Dark though she be
I find solace in her depths
I fall right in
Alongside her waves
No ripples I make
I am Ama

Bento Blessing

(British Columbia)
Sculpted love holding a thousand wishes
Of fortune, peace, wisdom
Spirit guided hands carve love
Messages from the ancient ones
Who straddle land and sea,
Those who know that wisdom like tendrils
Encircling ancient tombs
Wrap around our ankles, pages, and pens
Pushing paper
To form words
To spill thoughts
To bring the bento blessing to you.

Conversation

To hear a new world
She put her face in water
She does not want air
And all its nothingness
Its meaningless chatter
Floating on so-called breath.
She'd rather hear
The songs beneath
The dipping oars
Swishing fins
And whale calls.

Falling

She never really let go.
He held her right hand
As she fell through time
A million stars
Surrounding her
In a brilliant sky
Burning with new life.
She held on
And,
He never let go

First Wave

They didn't see it coming
That first wave
It wiped out the first
Of the three dragon suns
Leaving two forlorn
Hanging, alone.
When it was done
They walked back,
Across the barren land
Not holding hands.

The Tide Came

The tide rose that day
An unexpected swell
A wall of rock
That blocked off all light.
No-one expected it
But its time had come
Like clockwork
The Earth was done
And man,
Undone.

The Desert

A sickle moon rose
Above the three dragon suns
Here, dusk was day
And night, the morn.
She set out once more
In search of lore
For they needed tales,
Of how it was, before.
She pocketed them deep
And kept them high
Giddy with nostalgia
The desert, so dry
Had nothing to give.

Connection

He came back to earth
And she was waiting
Wearing lipstick
And nothing else.
Gravity held him down
And their
Cosmic connection
Held them,
Together.

Bath

In the rainbow
of the three dragon suns
She bathed in quiet,
Unmoved by the acrid air
Of the new planet.
Feet in the surf
Hands on her golden skin
She was in love with herself
A rare phenomenon
In this universe.

Sound

Sometimes,
The three dragon suns screamed
As thunderous rocks pulled past them.
This space was not silent
Humans could hear it.
Crackling cosmic storms
Whipping stellar winds
Heaving ice sheets
Melting tumbling glaciers.
Most humans remained inside.
Only the rangers, roamed free.

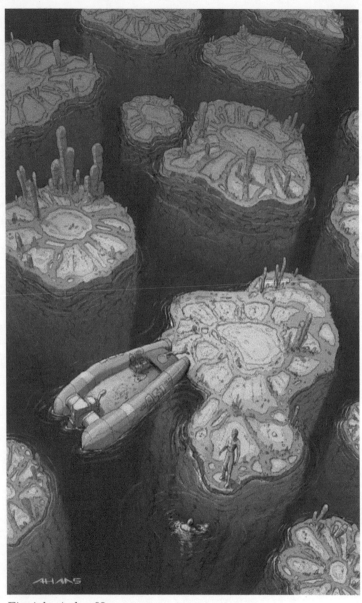

First in by Arthur Haas

First In

Standing atop the canyon
He looked down.
Below, his partner floated.
The waters had risen faster than expected
Catching --
People, animals, and things, unaware.
It all lay at the bottom now,
Deep below
In inky depths.

Under

Sometimes, he went under
Away from the three glazed suns
And their searing heat.
There, in writhing green depths
He would think about life before,
How green was of the surface,
And how the blue was under.
But alone, in the deep emerald depths
He touched slimy fronds
And saw translucent bulbs belch gas
To a lifeless top,
So silent it was below,
That he could remember nothing of before.

Jungleman by Arthur Haas

The Meeting by Arthur Haas

The Meeting

It was humid in the valley
And nets got stuck
With the dredging.
She dropped into the sludge
And eased the bug in place
Its slick proboscis
Sucked the sludge dry
Leaving slugs to writhe on sand.
Finished,
She melted up into the rover
And stopped thinking
About him.

Alignment

It was a red day.
A quiet grove of feather heads
Stood proud among bristle thorns.
The alignment was near
And all nature, forlorn
Would the three suns burn unceasingly?
Would charred creatures fall from the sky?
Would boiling black seas rise
And its black, black whales cry?
She gathered the feather heads
Arranged them in her basket
Neat little rows
Like little corpses, in one casket.

Data Collection

Listening to the waves
From inside a sealed hub
The men suck on their cigars
They can see
The ocean about them
Churning millions of underfed bodies
Pierced by fish bones.
The men had beamed down
From Beyond
To collect data on Earth
Looking about, they agreed
Nothing had changed
So,
They left.

The Other Sea

He stood on the shore
Of the Other Sea
And longed for her
A longing only surpassed
By the longing for Earth itself
The blue-green-grey-green-blue-blackness
Of Earth's seas.
Here,
The Other Sea was red
Like rushing blood
On a great gashing wound
The three suns hung over it
Like glaring eyes
Burning into black sand.

Air

In time the people came
To accept their place
Their underground, underling status
The foraging in the sludge
The acrid stench of alien life forms,
Rotting.
Above,
In air,
Those in power floated
Breathing thin atmosphere.
Their bodies unanchored
Hearts never heavy
Hands never dirty
Not even,
On the new planet.